# Two traditional tales

**The greedy dog**  page 2

**The ants and the grass-hopper**  page 9

Nelson

# The greedy dog

Once there was a greedy dog.
He liked to eat lots and
lots of meat.

One day he saw some meat in a shop.
He took the meat and ran out of the shop.

The greedy dog ran very fast.
Then he came to a river.
There was a plank over the river.

The greedy dog got
on the plank.
He looked down
into the water.
He saw a dog
with some meat.

"I will take the meat from that dog," said the greedy dog. "Then I will have two bits of meat."

So the greedy dog jumped
off the plank into the water.
But there was no dog in
the water after all.
And there was no meat.

The greedy dog opened his mouth.
His bit of meat fell out.
So the greedy dog did not get any meat after all.
But he did get very wet.

# The ants and the grass-hopper

It was summer.
The little ants were
hard at work.
They were getting lots of
food for the winter.

The grass-hopper was not hard at work.
He was playing in the sun.
He was not getting food for the winter.

"Why do you work so hard?"
he said to the ants.
"There is lots to eat.
Come and play with me."

"No," said the ants.
"We must get our food
for the winter."

So the ants went on
working and the grass-hopper
went on playing
in the sun.

Then the winter came.
It was cold and
there was no food.
But the ants had lots of food.

"We can play now," they said
to the grass-hopper.
But the grass-hopper was sad.
He had no food.

"If you play for us we will give you food," said the ants. "But next summer you must work as well."